Penguin Books
Physical Fitness

Physical Fitness

5BX 11-minute-a-day plan for men

XBX 12-minute-a-day plan for women

Two Series of Exercises
developed by
the Royal Canadian Air Force

Penguin Books

Penguin Books Ltd, Harmondsworth, Middlesex, England
Penguin Books, 40 West 23rd Street,
New York, New York 10010, U.S.A.
Penguin Books Australia Ltd, Ringwood, Victoria, Australia
Penguin Books Canada Ltd, 2801 John Street,
Markham, Ontario, Canada L3R 1B4
Penguin Books (N.Z.) Ltd, 182–190 Wairau Road,
Auckland 10, New Zealand

5BX first published by the R.C.A.F. 1958
XBX first published by the R.C.A.F. 1960
Published in Penguin Books 1964
Reprinted 1964, 1965, 1966, 1967 (twice), 1968, 1969, 1970 (twice),
1971 (three times), 1972, 1973, 1975 (twice), 1976, 1977 (twice),
1978 (twice), 1979, 1980, 1981, 1982, 1983 (twice)

Made and printed in Great Britain by
Hazell Watson & Viney Ltd, Aylesbury, Bucks
Set in Monotype Grotesque 215

Contents

Foreword

This is an age in which, even in the country, more and more people go everywhere on wheels. Keeping fit has become a universal problem. Though they may not be willing to spend time and money at a gymnasium and have no ambitions in the sphere of the 'body beautiful', very many people are nevertheless worried today about their figures and their general state of health.

The system of exercises detailed in this book presents an exceedingly simple answer to the problem. These plans were developed by the Royal Canadian Air Force in order to keep personnel at a peak of physical fitness, ready to face sudden demands for energy after long periods of inactivity. When they were made available to the general public, the two booklets of exercises contained in this volume rapidly became best-sellers all over North America. Their publication in Penguins will enable them to reach an even wider audience.

These exercises are specially designed for those who are pressed for time, whose work is mainly sedentary, and who have neither the space nor the taste for formal games or walks; for city-dwellers (in particular) who, even if they hardly ever go to the shops without a car, may occasionally have to sprint for a bus or climb stairs when the lift is out of order; and for those who are becoming aware of 'middle-aged spread' or of the strain of work, but are disinclined to take very strong action.

The 5BX and XBX plans, as these exercises are called, are graded progressively and the performer is not expected to go beyond the simpler movements at the beginning of the course until he or she can do them without difficulty in the time set. The pace of progress and the degree of fitness are entirely up to the performer. In this way it has been proved that adequate fitness can be achieved by easy stages, in very little space and without exaggerated exertion, at the cost of only a few minutes each day. Above all this system does not reach too high. It aims to provide the right degree of fitness for all normal purposes, without arousing any anxiety about Olympic standards of training.

5BX and XBX are ideal for anyone who simply wants to get fit, look fit, feel fit, and stay fit.

Acknowledgements

The R.C.A.F. acknowledges the contribution made to the preparation of the 5BX Pamphlet by W. A. R. Orban, Ph.D., Canadian physical education experts, and R.C.A.F. medical advisers, and to the preparation of the XBX Pamphlet by N. J. Ashton, B.Sc., M.S., Physical Education Specialist.

Introduction

Why You Should Be Fit

Research has shown that the physically fit person is able to withstand fatigue for longer periods than the unfit; that the physically fit person is better equipped to tolerate physical stress; that the physically fit person has a stronger and more efficient heart; and that there is a relationship between good mental alertness, absence of nervous tension, and physical fitness.

Remember that: (1) weak stomach muscles cause sagging abdomens; and (2) weak back muscles are a major cause of back pain.

There are countless reasons for being fit. *You* know how you feel. *Everyone* knows how you look. Regular exercise can improve your sense of well-being and your appearance. Fitness is necessary for the fullest enjoyment of living.

Weight Control

The major purpose of weight control is to reduce the amount of fat on the body and to increase the amount of muscle. It is, in reality, a

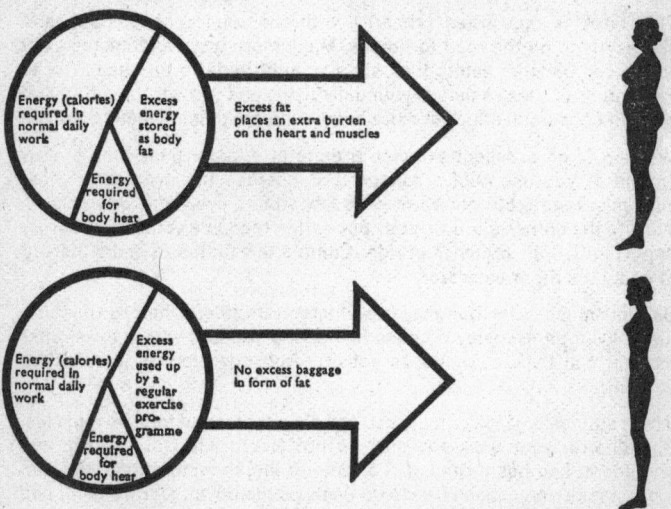

programme of fat control rather than weight control. This control can be exerted only by coupling a sensible dietary programme with a regular, balanced programme of exercise.

When we eat, the food is used, stored, or discarded. The body stores fuel, or calories, as fat. The more fuel we consume, and the less of it we use, then the more of it that is stored in the body in the form of fat. The human body is not like a car's petrol tank that will overflow when full. Our bodies accept all the calories that we put into them, and store those which we do not use.

For example, if you eat food that has a value of 3,000 calories and use only 2,600 of them in your activity, then the remaining 400 calories are stored in the body. Every time you accumulate about 4,000 of these calories you will notice an extra pound of weight on the scales.

When you exercise you burn calories. Energy used in this way will result in muscle development. As muscle is slightly heavier than fat, you may very well notice an increase in your weight rather than a reduction. However it must be stressed that this muscle weight is useful weight and will improve the way you look and feel.

Research has shown clearly that the most effective way of taking off weight and keeping it off is through a programme which combines exercise and diet.

Live To Be Fit and Be Fit To Live

This book is concerned primarily with the habits of exercise and diet as steps on the road to fitness. Many more ways and means exist which can become habits that will also contribute to this goal. Try to make some of these a part of your daily living and you will soon find that without conscious effort, or extra 'work', you are gaining many benefits.

Walking is an excellent exercise if done at a faster pace than a slow shuffle. If you use public transport, do not use the nearest or most convenient stop, but get on or off a few streets away and walk briskly. Walk to the corner shop or post box rather than use your car. At every opportunity, walk rather than ride. Climb a few flights of stairs instead of using the lift or escalator.

Use your muscles for lifting objects when you are able, rather than pushing them. Even an everyday practice like drying yourself with a towel after bathing can become a fitness activity. Rub down briskly rather than daubing.

While sitting at a desk or table you can aid posture and tone up muscles. Sit tall with your back straight; do not slump with round back and shoulders, and head forward. To tone up the shoulder girdle and arm muscles: sit erect, place hands on desk, palms down, elbows bent, and press down, trying to lift body from chair. Hold the pressure for a few seconds. Repeat two or three times a day.

When standing, sitting, or lying, tense the muscles of the abdomen and hold for about six seconds. Do this a few times each day. Constantly think of how you look, and walk tall and sit tall, always attempting to maintain a good postural position.

Rest, Relaxation, and Revitalization

It is just as important that your body receives adequate rest as it is that it be exercised. Sleep requirements vary from person to person and each person is his own best judge of these needs. The important thing is to awake refreshed and revitalized. A few tips on getting the most from your bedtime hours:

(1) keep the room as dark as possible;
(2) do not take your problems to bed with you – if you must think, think calm, restful thoughts;
(3) mild exercise before retiring may be helpful;
(4) if you are hungry, have a light snack or a warm, non-stimulating beverage.

Relaxation, both mental and physical, is becoming more and more essential in the fast moving, hurly-burly world in which we live. Many emotional tensions are reflected in physical tensions, both organic and muscular.

You can consciously reduce both forms of tension. Physically you can learn to relax muscle groups. A simple illustration is this: hold your hands in front of you, tighten up the muscles of the forearms so that the hands and fingers are straight, abruptly relax them so that the hands fall limply. Try this with other muscles – tighten – then relax. Stretch, writhe, and wriggle yourself into a relaxed state.

For mental relaxation try consciously to think pleasant and restful thoughts, ignoring for a while the troubles of the day. Healthy forms of recreation (picnics, golf, etc.) are fine ways to release not only the physical tensions, but some of the mental ones as well.

Exercise and the Heart

There are many misconceptions about exercise and its effect upon the heart. 'Exercise is harmful.' Nonsense. There is no evidence to support this contention. There is a large body of opinion which holds that exercise, appropriate to age and physical condition, continued through your life span will help to reduce the possibility of heart and blood vessel disease. Exercise, in mild form of course, is recommended as part of the recuperative phase in cases of heart or coronary disease. Evidence is also on hand that indicates exercise is beneficial to the function of the cardio-vascular system.

A healthy heart can obtain many benefits from a good conditioning programme. Research has shown that the heart of a trained person has a smaller acceleration of pulse rate under stress, and that it returns more rapidly to its normal rate afterwards than that of an untrained person; that it pumps more blood per beat at rest, and that it can pump more during exercise; that it has more richly developed small blood vessels supplying the heart muscle and that it functions more efficiently. An efficient cardio-vascular system means a better supply of food and oxygen to the muscles (as blood is the carrier of these items) and a quicker recuperation after exertion, be it work, play, or exercise.

A cautionary note: persons over thirty-five years of age, and anyone who suspects that they may have something wrong with their heart, should have a thorough medical examination before engaging in a vigorous exercise programme. Experts have noted that a heart already injured by disease will suffer extra abuse through extreme forms of exercise. Sudden violent exertion after a period of inactivity is to be avoided.

Exercise, Strength, and Endurance

The strength and endurance of the body can be increased through regular exercise. Such improvements are primarily localized in the muscles and organs which are exercised – one cannot strengthen the arms and shoulders by exercising the legs. To improve the condition of all muscles one must undertake a programme which will provide them all with work.

The strength of a muscle is measured by the amount of force that that muscle can exert and is dependent upon the size and number of muscle fibres that can be brought into action at any one time and the frequency of the nerve impulses to them.

Endurance is concerned with the ability to repeat an action over and over again, or to sustain a muscular contraction.

Since the fuel for muscular contraction is carried in the blood, endurance is chiefly dependent upon the functioning of the cardio-respiratory system, (heart, blood vessels, and lungs – that is, the ability of the body to transport food and oxygen to the muscles, and waste products away from them, efficiently.

The human body requires proper use to function efficiently and endure. The body is very different from a machine that wears out with use. Most persons have noted how the muscles of an arm or a leg in a cast become smaller and weaker the longer the arm or leg remains so encased. While this is a dramatic example it is in effect what happens to the muscles of the body in a milder way when these muscles are not used enough. Exercise over and above the normal demands of daily living is essential to the development of an efficient, strong, and durable body.

The resultant more pleasing appearance and sense of well-being are added benefits that cannot be overlooked.

Caution – before you start

If you have any doubt as to your capability to undertake this programme, *see your medical adviser*. You should not perform fast, vigorous, or highly competitive physical activity without gradually developing, and continuously maintaining, an adequate level of physical fitness, particularly if you are over the age of 30.

The 5BX Plan for Men

The 5BX Plan for Men

Physical Fitness

The human body is made up mainly of bone, muscle, and fat. Some 639 different muscles account for about 45 per cent of the body weight. Each of these muscles has four distinct and measurable qualities which are of interest to us:

(1) it can produce force which can be measured as strength of muscle;
(2) it can store energy which permits it to work for extended periods of time independent of circulation – this is generally referred to as *muscular endurance*;
(3) it can shorten at varying rates. This is called *speed of contraction*;
(4) it can be stretched and will recoil. This is called the *elasticity of muscle*.

The combination of these four qualities of muscle is referred to as *muscular power*.

If muscles are to function efficiently, they must be continually supplied with energy fuel. This is accomplished by the blood which carries the energy fuel from lungs and digestive system to the muscles. The blood is forced through the blood vessels by the heart. The combined capacity to supply energy fuels to the working muscles is called *organic power*.

The capacity and efficiency with which your body can function depends on the degree of development of both your muscular and organic power through regular exercise. However, the level to which you can develop these powers is influenced by such factors as the type of body you have, the food you eat, presence or absence of disease, rest and sleep. You are physically fit only when you have adequately developed your muscular and organic power to perform with the highest possible efficiency.

How Fit Should You Be?

Heredity and health determine the top limits to which your physical capacity can be developed. This is known as your potential physical capacity. This potential capacity varies from individual to individual. Most of us, for example, could train for a lifetime and never come close to running a four-minute mile simply because we weren't 'built' for it. The top level at which you can perform physically right now is called your 'acquired capacity' because it has been acquired or developed through physical activity in your daily routines.

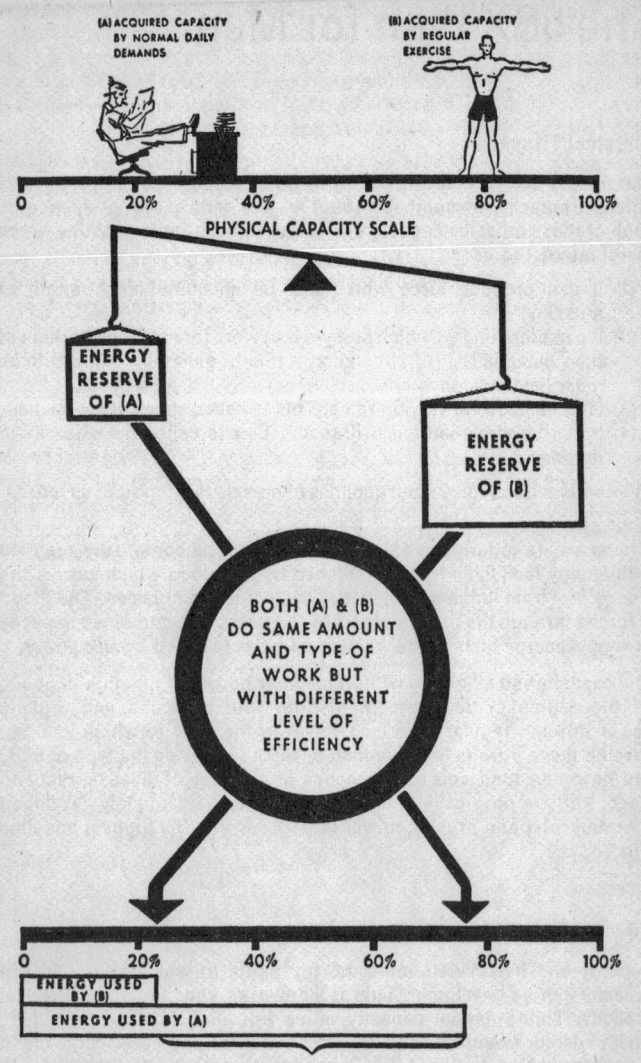

The amount of extra energy left over to enjoy recreational activities by an individual (B) who takes regular exercise

Your body, like a car, functions most efficiently well below its acquired capacity. A car, for example, driven at its top speed of, say, 110 miles per hour uses more petrol per mile than when it is driven around 50–60 miles per hour, which is well below its capacity. Your body functions in the same way, in that the ratio of work performed to energy expended is better when it functions well below acquired capacity.

You can avoid wastage of energy by acquiring a level of physical capacity well above the level required to perform your normal daily tasks. This can be accomplished by supplementing your daily physical activity with a balanced exercise programme performed regularly. Your capacity increases as you progressively increase the load on your muscular and organic systems. Exercise will increase physical endurance and stamina thus providing a greater reserve of energy for leisure-time activities.

The Contribution of Sports and Other Activities to Basic Physical Efficiency

Just as a balanced diet must be composed of a sufficient quantity of the proper kinds of foods to ensure that nutritional requirements are adequately met, so should a balanced physical activity programme be composed of a sufficient quantity of the proper kind of physical activity so that all the important parts of the body are adequately exercised.

The parts of the body that require special attention are the muscles of the shoulders and arms, abdomen and back, legs, and the heart, lungs, and blood vessels.

No single sport provides a truly balanced development for all parts of the body. This can only be acquired by regular participation in a number of carefully selected sports. Such participation, however, is not possible for the average person for a number of reasons – availability of play opportunity, time, expense. The most practical physical fitness scheme for most of us is participation in one or two sports supplemented by a balanced set of exercises. The 5BX programme has been designed to bring physical fitness within the reach of any healthy man who is willing to devote eleven minutes a day to a simple but balanced set of exercises.

Common Sense About Exercise

'It won't do you any good to exercise unless you do it until it hurts', the saying goes. This is absolutely false. Although you may get some benefit from doing exercises until 'it hurts', this is not necessary in order to acquire an adequate level of physical fitness. As a matter of fact, greater benefits can be derived from exercise by avoiding stiffness and soreness.

Physical efficiency comparisons

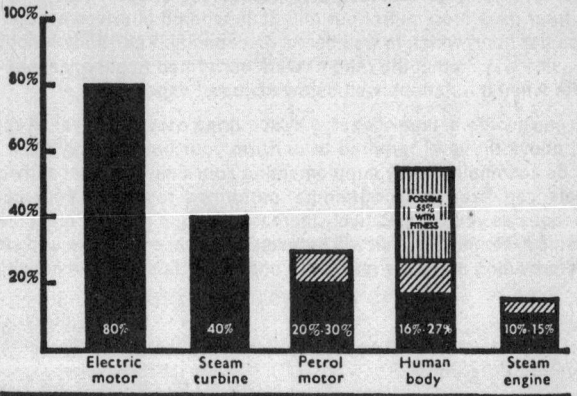

The efficiency of the human body compares poorly with the modern machine. However, through regular exercise its efficiency can be considerably increased

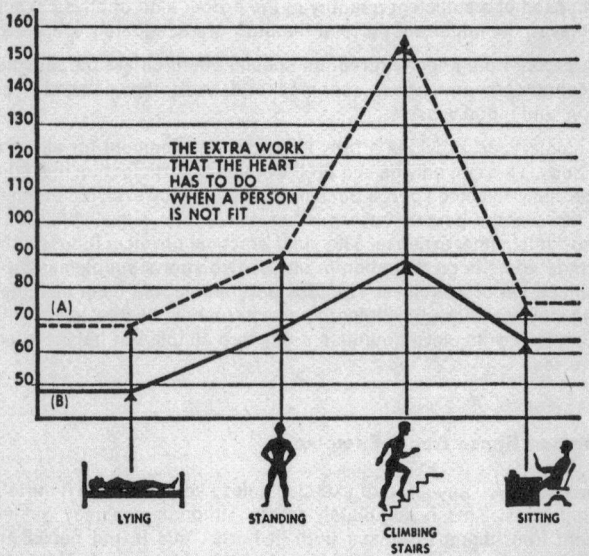

This graph illustrates the number of heart-beats required for different routine activities by a human being, (A) before and (B) after a regular vigorous exercise programme

There are basically two ways in which you can avoid discomfort and still develop high levels of physical capacity:

(1) warm up properly before participating in any strenuous physical activity such as sprinting, handball, tennis, etc.;
(2) start any training programme at a low level of activity and work up by easy stages.

Warming Up

The 5BX Plan was designed so that no additional warm-up is necessary in order to receive its maximum benefits.

The older one is, the more necessary proper warming up becomes to avoid 'strained' muscles. The 5BX Plan has a built-in method of warm-up. This is achieved in two ways:

(1) by the arrangement of the exercises; and
(2) by the manner in which these exercises are performed.

For example the first exercise is a stretching and loosening exercise which limbers up the large muscles of the body. In addition, this exercise should be started very slowly and easily, with a gradual increase in speed and vigour.

Let us see how this principle applies to Exercise One (see p. 27), which requires you to touch the floor. You should not force yourself to do it on the first attempt, but rather start by pushing down very gently and slowly as far as you can without undue strain – then on each succeeding try push down a little harder, and, at the same time, do the exercise a little faster so that by the end of two minutes you are touching the floor and moving at the necessary speed. All the exercises can be performed in this manner.

If you choose to do the exercises in the morning, and are a slow starter, as soon as the alarm rings, stretch, arch your back, lift your legs, and start riding your bicycle.

What is the 5BX Plan?

The 5BX Plan is composed of six charts arranged in progression. Each chart is composed of five exercises which are always performed in the same order and in the same maximum time limit, but, as you progress from chart to chart, there are slight changes in each basic exercise with a gradual demand for more effort.

A sample rating scale of Chart Three is reproduced on page 23 and is to be used in the following way:

Level

These are the physical capacity levels, each indicated by a letter of the alphabet.

Exercises

Exercises One, Two, Three, and Four apply to the first four exercises described and illustrated on the following pages. The column headed 1 represents Exercise One (toe touch), etc. The figures in each column indicate the number of times that each exercise is to be repeated in the time allotted for that exercise. Exercise Five is running on the spot. Two activities may be substituted for it, however, and if you prefer you may run or walk the recommended distance in the required time in place of the stationary run of Exercise Five.

Minutes for Each Exercise

The allotted time for each exercise is noted at the bottom of the exercise columns. These times remain the same throughout all the charts. Total time for exercises One to Five is eleven minutes.

Note: It is important that the exercises at any level be completed in eleven minutes. *However, it is likely that in the early stages, an individual will complete certain exercises in less than the allotted time while others may require longer.* In these circumstances the times allotted for individual exercises may be varied within the total eleven-minute period.

How Far Should You Progress?

The level of physical capacity to which you should progress is determined by your 'age group'. Levels for flying crew (peak physical fitness) are listed separately. The levels in this plan are based on the expectation of average individuals, and this means there will be some men who are capable of progressing beyond the level indicated, and, on the other hand, there will be persons who will never attain this average level.

Use the goals as guides, and apply them with common sense.

Here Are a Few Tips

When you start, defeat the first desire to skip a day; then defeat all such desires as they occur. This exercise programme has plenty of bite; the longer you do it the more you will enjoy it.

As you progress well into the programme you may find certain levels almost impossible to complete in eleven minutes – but work hard at that

Chart 3

Age Groups

12 yrs maintains D+
13 yrs maintains C+
14 yrs maintains B+
35–9 yrs maintains B
40–44 yrs maintains C

Flying Crew

Age 40–44 maintains A+
Age 45–9 maintains B

| Level | EXERCISE | | | | | 1 mile run | 2 mile walk |
	1	2	3	4	5	In minutes	
A+	30	32	47	24	550	8	25
A	30	31	45	22	540	8	25
A−	30	30	43	21	525	8	25
B+	28	28	41	20	510	$8\frac{1}{4}$	26
B	28	27	39	19	500	$8\frac{1}{4}$	26
B−	28	26	37	18	490	$8\frac{1}{4}$	26
C+	26	25	35	17	480	$8\frac{1}{2}$	27
C	26	24	34	17	465	$8\frac{1}{2}$	27
C−	26	23	33	16	450	$8\frac{1}{2}$	27
D+	24	22	31	15	430	$8\frac{3}{4}$	28
D	24	21	30	15	415	$8\frac{3}{4}$	28
D−	24	20	29	15	400	$8\frac{3}{4}$	29
Minutes for each exercise	2	1	1	1	6		

1 Feet astride, arms upward. Touch floor 6 ins. outside left foot, again between feet and press once, then 6 ins. outside right foot, bend backwards as far as possible, repeat, reverse direction after half the number of counts.

2 Back lying, feet 6 ins. apart, arms clasped behind head. Sit up to vertical position, keep feet on floor; hook feet under chair, etc., only if necessary.

3 Front lying, hands interlocked behind the back. Lift head, shoulders, chest and both legs as high as possible. Keep legs straight, and raise chest and both thighs completely off floor.

4 Front lying, hands under the shoulders palms flat on floor. Touch chin to floor in front of hands – touch forehead to floor behind hands before returning to up position. There are three definite movements, chin, forehead, arms straightened. *Do not* do in one continuous movement.

5 Stationary run. (Count a step each time left foot touches floor.) Lift feet approximately 4 ins. off floor. After every 75 steps do 10 'half knee bends'. Repeat sequence until required number of steps is completed. Half knee bends. Feet together, hands on hips, knees bent to form an angle of about 110 degrees. Do not bend knees past a right angle. Straighten to upright position, raising heels off floor, return to starting position each time. Keep feet in contact with floor – the back upright and straight at all times.

level (it may take some days or even weeks) and suddenly you will find yourself sailing ahead again.

Counting the steps in Exercise Five can be difficult. You can lose count very easily at times. If you have this problem, here is an easy way to overcome it. Divide the total number of steps required by seventy-five and note the answer – place a row of buttons, corresponding in number to this answer, on a handy table or chair. Now count off your first seventy-five steps – do your ten required movements – and move the first button. Repeat until all the buttons have been removed, finishing up with any left-over steps. For diversity, occasionally an exercise from the previous chart may be substituted.

How To Begin

Check your daily schedule and determine the time most convenient for you to do the exercises. It should be the same time each day.
   Here are some suggested times:
   (1) before breakfast;
   (2) late morning or afternoon, at your place of employment;
   (3) after your regular recreational period;
   (4) in the evening just before you retire.
Regardless of the time you choose *start today.*

Maximum Rate of Progression Through Chart One

20 years or under, at least one day at each level
20–29 years, at least two days at each level
30–39 years, at least four days at each level
40–49 years, at least seven days at each level
50–59 years, at least eight days at each level
60 years and over, at least ten days at each level

(If you feel stiff or sore, or if you are unduly breathless at any time, ease up and slow down your rate of progression. This is particularly applicable to the older age groups.)

A Note of Caution

Even if you feel able to start at a high level and progress at a faster rate than indicated – *don't do it* – start at the bottom of Chart One and work up from level to level as recommended.

For best results from 5BX the exercises must be done *regularly.* Remember, it may take you, 6, 8, 10 months or more of daily exercises to attain the level recommended for you, but once you have attained it, only three periods of exercise per week will maintain this level of physical capacity. If for any reason (illness, etc.) you stop doing 5BX regularly and you wish to begin again, *do not* recommence at the level you had attained previously.

Do drop back several levels until you find one you can do without undue strain. After a period of inactivity of longer than two months, or one month if caused by illness, it is recommended that you start again at Chart One.

How to Progress

Start at the lowest physical capacity level of Chart One (D−). Repeat each exercise in the allotted time or do the five exercises in eleven minutes. Move upwards on the same chart to the next level, D, only after you can complete all the required movements at your present level within eleven minutes. Continue to progress upwards in this manner until you can complete all the required movements at level A+ within eleven minutes. Now start at the bottom of Chart Two (D−), and continue in this fashion upwards through the levels, and from chart to chart, until you reach the level for your age group; e.g. age 35–9 (B Chart Three) does 32 levels from D− on Chart One to B on Chart Three.

Chart 1

Physical capacity rating scale

Age Groups

6 yrs maintains B
7 yrs maintains A

Level	EXERCISE					½ mile run	1 mile walk
	1	2	3	4	5	In minutes	
A+	20	18	22	13	400	5½	17
A	18	17	20	12	375	5½	17
A−	16	15	18	11	335	5½	17
B+	14	13	16	9	320	6	18
B	12	12	14	8	305	6	18
B−	10	11	12	7	280	6	18
C+	8	9	10	6	260	6½	19
C	7	8	9	5	235	6½	19
C−	6	7	8	4	205	6½	19
D+	4	5	6	3	175	7	20
D	3	4	5	3	145	7½	21
D−	2	3	4	2	100	8	21
Minutes for each exercise	2	1	1	1	6		

1 Feet astride, arms upward. Forward bend to floor touching then stretch upward and backward bend. Do not strain to keep knees straight.

2 Back lying, feet 6 ins. apart, arms at sides. Sit up just far enough to see your heels. Keep legs straight, head and shoulders must clear the floor.

3 Front lying, palms placed under the thighs. Raise head and one leg, repeat using legs alternately. Keep leg straight at the knee, thighs must clear the palms. (Count one each time second leg touches floor.)

4 Front lying, hands under the shoulders, palms flat on the floor. Straighten arms lifting upper body, keeping the knees on the floor. Bend arms to lower body. Keep body straight from the knees, arms must be fully extended, chest must touch floor to complete one movement.

5 Stationary run. (Count a step each time left foot touches floor.) Lift feet approximately 4 ins. off floor. Every 75 steps do 10 'scissor jumps'. Repeat this sequence until required number of steps is completed.
Scissor jumps. Stand with right leg and left arm extended forward, and left leg and right arm extended backward. Jump up – change position of arms and legs before landing. Repeat (arms shoulder high).

Exercise 1

Exercise 2

Exercise 3

Exercise 4

Exercise 5

Chart 2

Physical capacity rating scale

Age Groups

  8 yrs maintains D—

  9 yrs maintains C—

 10 yrs maintains B—

 11 yrs maintains A—

45–9 yrs maintains A+

50–60 yrs maintains C+

Level	EXERCISE					1 mile run	2 mile walk
	1	2	3	4	5	In minutes	
A+	30	23	33	20	500	9	30
A	29	21	31	19	485	9	31
A—	28	20	29	18	470	9	32
B+	26	18	27	17	455	9½	33
B	24	17	25	16	445	9½	33
B—	22	16	23	15	440	9½	33
C+	20	15	21	14	425	10	34
C	19	14	19	13	410	10	34
C—	18	13	17	12	395	10	34
D+	16	12	15	11	380	10½	35
D	15	11	14	10	360	10½	35
D—	14	10	13	9	335	10½	35
Minutes for each exercise	2	1	1	1	6		

1 Feet astride, arms upward. Touch floor and press (bounce) once then stretch upward and backward bend.

2 Back lying, feet 6 ins. apart, arms at sides. 'Sit up' to vertical position, keep feet on floor even if it is necessary to hook them under a chair.

3 Front lying, palms placed under thighs. Raise head, shoulders, and both legs. Keep legs straight, both thighs must clear the palms.

4 Front lying, hands under the shoulders, palms flat on floor. Straighten arms to lift body with only palms and toes on the floor. Back straight. Chest must touch floor for each completed movement after arms have been fully extended.

5 Stationary run. (Count a step each time left foot touches floor.) Lift feet approximately 4 ins. off floor. After every 75 steps, do 10 'astride jumps'. Repeat this sequence until required number of steps is completed.

Astride jumps. Feet together, arms at side. Jump and land with feet astride and arms raised sideways to slightly above shoulder height. Return with a jump to the starting position for count of one. Keep arms straight.

Exercise 1

Exercise 2

Exercise 3

Exercise 4

Exercise 5

Chart 3

Age Groups

- 12 yrs maintains D+
- 13 yrs maintains C+
- 14 yrs maintains B+
- 35–9 yrs maintains B
- 40–44 yrs maintains C

Flying Crew

- 40–44 yrs maintains A+
- 45–9 yrs maintains B

Level	EXERCISE					1 mile run	2 mile walk
	1	2	3	4	5	In minutes	
A+	30	32	47	24	550	8	25
A	30	31	45	22	540	8	25
A−	30	30	43	21	525	8	25
B+	28	28	41	20	510	8¼	26
B	28	27	39	19	500	8¼	26
B−	28	26	37	18	490	8¼	26
C+	26	25	35	17	480	8½	27
C	26	24	34	17	465	8½	27
C−	26	23	33	16	450	8½	27
D+	24	22	31	15	430	8¾	28
D	24	21	30	15	415	8¾	28
D−	24	20	29	15	400	8¾	29
Minutes for each exercise	2	1	1	1	6		

1 Feet astride, arms upward. Touch floor 6 ins. outside left foot, again between feet and press once, then 6 ins. outside right foot, bend backward as far as possible, repeat, reverse direction after half the number of counts.

2 Back lying, feet 6 ins. apart, arms clasped behind head. Sit up to vertical position, keep feet on floor, hook feet under chair, etc., only if necessary.

3 Front lying, hands interlocked behind the back. Lift head, shoulders, chest, and both legs as high as possible. Keep legs straight, and raise chest and both thighs completely off floor.

4 Front lying, hands under the shoulders, palms flat on floor. Touch chin to floor in front of hands – touch forehead to floor behind hands before returning to up position. There are three definite movements, chin, forehead, arms straightened. *Do not* do in one continuous movement.

5 Stationary run. (Count a step each time left foot touches floor.) Lift feet approximately 4 ins. off floor. After every 75 steps do 10 'half knee bends'. Repeat this sequence until required number of steps is completed.

Half knee bends. Feet together, hands on hips, knees bent to form an angle of about 110 degrees; do not bend knees past a right angle. Straighten to upright position, raising heels off floor, return to starting position each time. Keep feet in contact with floor – the back upright and straight at all times.

Exercise 1

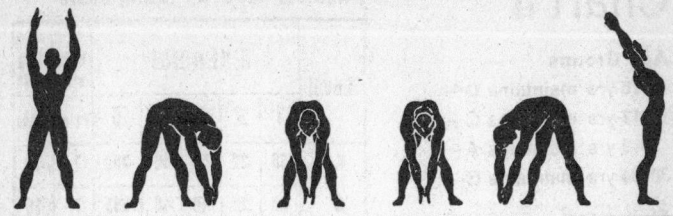

Exercise 2

Exercise 3

Exercise 4

Exercise 5

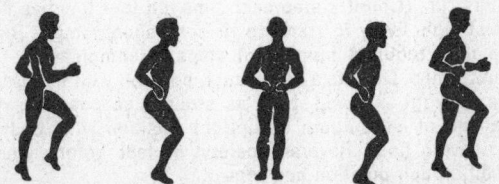

Chart 4

Physical capacity rating scale

Age Groups

15 yrs maintains D—
16–17 yrs maintains C+
25–9 yrs maintains A+
30–34 yrs maintains C—

Flying Crew

30–34 yrs maintains B
35–9 yrs maintains C—

Level	EXERCISE					1 mile run	2 mile walk
	1	2	3	4	5	In minutes	
A+	30	22	50	42	400	7	19
A	30	22	49	40	395	7	19
A—	30	22	49	37	390	7	19
B+	28	21	47	34	380	7¼	20
B	28	21	46	32	375	7¼	20
B—	28	21	46	30	365	7¼	20
C+	26	19	44	28	355	7½	21
C	26	19	43	26	345	7½	21
C—	26	19	43	24	335	7½	21
D+	24	18	41	21	325	7¾	23
D	24	18	40	19	315	7¾	23
D—	24	18	40	17	300	7¾	23
Minutes for each exercise	2	1	1	1	6		

1 Feet astride, arms upward. Touch floor outside left foot, between feet, press once, then outside right foot, circle, bend backwards as far as possible, reverse directions after half the number of counts. Keep arms above head and make full circle, bending backward past vertical each time.

2 Back lying, legs straight, feet together, arms straight overhead. Sit up and touch the toes keeping the arms and legs straight. Use chair to hook feet under only if necessary. Keep arms in contact with the sides of the head throughout the movement.

3 Front lying, hands and arms stretched sideways. Lift head, shoulders, arms, chest, and both legs as high as possible. Keep legs straight, raise chest and both thighs completely off floor.

4 Front lying, palms of hands flat on floor, approximately 1 foot from ears directly to side of head. Straighten arms to lift body. Chest must touch floor for each completed movement.

5 Stationary run. (Count a step each time left foot touches floor.) Lift knees waist high. Every 75 steps do 10 'semi-squat jumps'. Repeat this sequence until required number of steps is completed.

Semi-squat umps. Drop to a half crouch position with hands on knees and arms straight, keeping back as straight as possible, right foot slightly ahead of left. Jump to upright position with body straight and feet leaving floor. Reverse position of feet before landing. Return to half crouch position and repeat.

Exercise 1

Exercise 2

Exercise 3

Exercise 4

Exercise 5

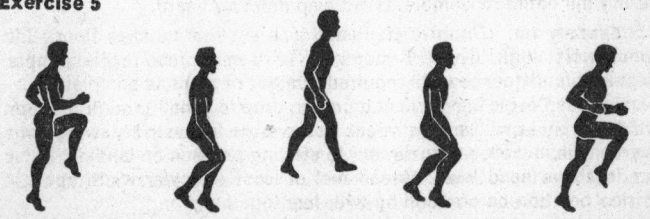

Chart 5

Physical capacity rating scale

Age Group
18–25 yrs maintains C

Flying Crew
Under 25 yrs maintains B+
25–9 yrs maintains D+

Level	EXERCISE					1 mile run
	1	2	3	4	5	Mins : Secs
A+	30	40	50	44	500	6 : 00
A	30	39	49	43	485	6 : 06
A–	30	38	48	42	475	6 : 09
B+	28	36	47	40	465	6 : 12
B	28	35	46	39	455	6 : 15
B–	28	34	45	38	445	6 : 21
C+	26	32	44	36	435	6 : 27
C	26	31	43	35	420	6 : 33
C–	26	30	42	34	410	6 : 39
D+	24	28	41	32	400	6 : 45
D	24	27	40	31	385	6 : 51
D–	24	26	39	30	375	7 : 00
Minutes for each exercise	2	1	1	1	6	

1 Feet astride, arms upward, hands clasped, arms straight. Touch floor outside left foot, between feet, press once, then outside right foot, circle bend backwards as far as possible. Reverse direction after half the number of counts.

2 Back lying, legs straight, feet together, hands clasped behind head. Sit up and raise legs in bent position, at same time twist to touch right elbow to left knee. This completes one movement. Alternate the direction of twist each time. Keep feet off floor when elbow touches knee.

3 Front lying, arms extended overhead. Raise arms, head, chest, and both legs as high as possible. Keep legs and arms straight, chest and both thighs completely off floor.

4 Front lying, hands under shoulders, palms flat on floor. Push off floor and clap hands before returning to starting position. Keep body straight during the entire movement. Hand clap must be heard.

5 Stationary run. (Count a step each time left foot touches floor.) Lift knees waist high. Every 75 steps do 10 'semi-spread eagle jumps'. Repeat this sequence until required number of steps is completed.
Semi-spread eagle jumps. Feet together, drop to a half crouch position hands on knees with arms straight. Jump up to feet astride, swing arms overhead in mid air, return directly to starting position on landing. Raise hands above head level, spread feet at least shoulder width apart in astride position before landing with feet together.

Exercise 1

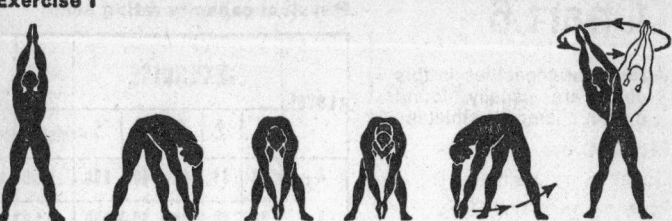

Exercise 2

Exercise 3

Exercise 4

Exercise 5

Chart 6

Physical capacities in this chart are usually found only in champion athletes

Level	EXERCISE					1 mile run
	1	2	3	4	5	Mins : Secs
A+	30	50	40	40	600	5 : 00
A	30	48	39	39	580	5 : 03
A−	30	47	38	38	555	5 : 09
B+	28	45	37	36	530	5 : 12
B	28	44	36	35	525	5 : 18
B−	28	43	35	34	515	5 : 24
C+	26	41	34	32	505	5 : 27
C	26	40	33	31	495	5 : 33
C−	26	39	32	30	485	5 : 39
D+	24	37	31	28	475	5 : 45
D	24	36	30	27	460	5 : 51
D−	24	35	29	26	450	6 : 00
Minutes for each exercise	2	1	1	1	6	

1 Feet astride, arms upward, hands reverse clasped, arms straight. Touch floor outside left foot, between feet, press once, then outside right foot, circle bend backwards as far as possible. Reverse direction after half the number of counts. Keep hands tightly reverse clasped at all times.

2 Back lying, legs straight, feet together, arms straight over the head. Sit up and at the same time lift both legs to touch the toes in a pike (V) position. Keep feet together, legs and arms straight, all of the upper back and legs clear floor, fingers touch toes each time.

3 Front lying, arms extended over head. Raise arms, head, chest, and both legs as high as possible then press back once. Keep legs and arms straight – chest and both thighs completely off floor.

4 Front lying, hands under shoulders, palms flat on floor. Push off floor and slap chest before returning to starting position. Keep body straight during the entire movement, chest slap must be heard.

5 Stationary run. (Count a step each time left foot touches floor. Lift knees waist high.) Every 75 steps do 10 'jack jumps'. Repeat this until required number of steps is completed.
Jack jumps. Feet together, knees bent. Sit on heels, finger tips touch floor. Jump up, raise legs waist high, keep legs straight and touch toes in mid air. Keep legs straight, raise feet level to 'standing waist height'. Touch toes each time.

Exercise 1

Exercise 2

Exercise 3

Exercise 4

Exercise 5

The XBX Plan for Women

The XBX Plan for Women

Your Appearance

Your appearance is controlled by the bony frame of your body, and by the proportions of fat and muscle which you have added to it. You cannot do anything about your skeleton, but you can, and should, do something about the fat and muscle.

All of us require a certain amount of fat on and in our bodies for functional reasons. Fat softens the bony contours of the body; it helps to keep the body temperature constant; and it acts as an energy storage vault. Fat appears in layers on the outside of the body, covers and lines the internal organs – the heart and blood vessels, for example – and it also makes up a part of muscle.

Except for certain neurotic or glandular conditions, people are over-fat because they over-eat and under-exercise.

Muscle is the other controllable factor in the appearance. When we are young we are fairly active; the muscles of our bodies are used and they retain that pleasing firmness – muscle tone. The less we exercise muscles the softer and more flabby they become. They become small with disuse, less elastic, and much weaker. Much of what is considered fatness in the abdominal region is nothing more than weak stomach muscles which permit the internal organs to sag forward. Your muscles perform the same function as a girdle – keep them as resilient as your foundation garment.

Because the condition of your muscles is so important to the way you look and feel, diet alone is not the best method for trying to improve your body measurements. The best method is a combination of diet and exercise. A thigh that is made up of little muscle and a lot of fat may have the same measurement as one that has firm muscle and a light fat layer, but – let's face it – it is just not the same thigh.

Do not confuse good muscle tone with bulky, unsightly muscles. The XBX is designed to firm your muscles – not to convert you into a muscled woman.

Diet

For many women, the knowledge that they have gained a few pounds, or added a few inches, causes what may be called the 'diet reflex'. Without pause to consult a medical expert they resort immediately to their favourite diet, which is more usually a fast. If you wish to go on a stringent diet – consult your doctor first.

As a rule you can avoid the need to resort to a strict reduction of food intake by the constant use of sensible dietary habits. In the normal individual, fat is added to the body very slowly. It may be several weeks or even months before you notice this gradual accumulation. You cannot hope to take this fat off and keep it off without making subtle changes in eating and exercise habits. After a 'crash diet', you will undoubtedly return to your old habits and in a few weeks you will note that *it* is back again once more.

A slight change in diet (along with XBX) can take off, and keep off, several pounds of excess fat over a period of time. For example, if you eat bread with your meals, eat one slice less; add a little less sugar, or none at all, to your tea or coffee. The calories so avoided each day add up to several thousand in a few months and may be the difference between the way you look and feel and the way you would like to look and feel. By the time you have arrived at the condition you desire your habits will have been changed enough so that you will probably not slip back into the old ones.

What You Can Do About Fitness

Unless you are engaged in a full-time programme of conditioning for athletic endeavours you should take part in some form of active exercise.

The average woman is engaged in one of three activities daily – school, employment, or housework. None of these provides the balanced activity for the body that is desirable for good physical fitness. Housework, for example, though it may involve a good deal of hard physical labour, does not take into account the flexibility of the muscles, nor does it work all the muscles of the body. Day after day you do the same things. The muscles that work get plenty of exercise; the others get little or none.

The same facts that are true of housework also hold true for most sports. Sports make specific contributions to fitness but do not condition the whole body. Most people taking part in a recreational sport do not pursue it vigorously enough to develop adequate levels of fitness. Before they become completely effective, even those sports which can produce all-round fitness require more skill than the average person possesses and more time than the average person can devote to them.

No matter what you do in your daily life you probably need a good, balanced programme of exercise which will enable you to become the person you want to be.

Why XBX Was Developed

Research has indicated that everyone – male and female, young and old – is in need of some form of regular, vigorous, physical activity. As more and more labour-saving devices are put into general use, as more and more people watch more and more television, films, and sports events, the amount of physical effort expended by the average person decreases continually.

An analysis of the exercise needs of Canadians was conducted by R.C.A.F. specialists and led to the development of the 5BX programme for men. XBX is the complementary programme for women.

The R.C.A.F. analysis indicated three major deterrents to regular exercise:

(1) a great majority of people would like to exercise, but do not know how to go about it – what to do, how to do it, how often, how to progress, or how far to progress;

(2) most exercise programmes call for the use of equipment and gymnasiums which are not always available; and

(3) most exercise programmes call for a great expenditure of time, which most people cannot spare.

Clearly a programme which resolves these problems is required.

The XBX tells you what to do, where to start, how fast you progress, and how far you should progress to achieve a desirable level of physical fitness. It requires no equipment and very little space, and takes only twelve minutes a day.

How XBX Was Developed

XBX is the product of extensive research into the problems of physical fitness for girls and women, the research having been conducted at several R.C.A.F. stations and in the later stages having included sections of the civilian population. Over 600 girls and women of all ages participated in the project and the R.C.A.F. is indebted to them for their contributions to the programme.

The first step in the project was the administration of a series of physical fitness tests. The tests included an examination of muscular strength and endurance, testing of heart response to activity, and measurement of fat layers. From the results of these tests the physical fitness needs of women were analysed. Experiments were carried out with a wide variety of exercises to determine those most effective in producing the desired results. Many of these exercises were discarded as ineffectual. The ten exercises of XBX provided the most balanced and effective programme.

The time limits for each exercise were varied until the optimum time for good results was determined, and the tests were conducted to arrive at the number of times each exercise could be done, and should be done, within the time limits.

Several hundred women used the first experimental exercise programmes and periodic tests showed that XBX was an effective plan to improve levels of general fitness.

The programme was then distributed to groups and to individuals across Canada for further trial and comment. Further modifications in the plan were made on the basis of this final field trial. The results of this research are presented in this book – the R.C.A.F. XBX Plan for Physical Fitness.

What the XBX Plan Is

The XBX Plan is a physical fitness programme composed of four charts of ten exercises, arranged in progressive order of difficulty. The ten exercises on each chart are always performed in the same order, and in the same maximum time limits.

The charts are divided into levels. There are 48 levels in all, 12 in each chart. The levels are numbered consecutively, starting with 1 at the bottom of Chart One and ending with 48 at the top of Chart Four.

In addition to the regular exercises, two supplementary exercises are available for Charts One, Two, and Three. These exercises are for the muscles of the feet and ankles and for those muscles which assist in the maintenance of good posture.

How XBX Works

Any exercise plan or programme should work on the basis of an easy start and gradual progression. As physical fitness improves, the work load is increased. The XBX approach to exercise follows these principles. XBX incorporates two methods to make the work load greater:

  (1) the time limit for each exercise remains the same in all charts, but the number of times the exercise is performed within this time limit is increased at each level within each chart; and
  (2) the exercises are made more difficult from each chart to the next higher one.

On each chart you do the same exercises at each of the twelve levels but increase the number of times you do them. As you move to the next higher chart the exercises are basically the same but have been modified and made slightly more demanding.

The XBX has been planned for gradual, painless progression. Follow the plan as outlined in the booklet; do not skip levels; do not progress faster than is recommended.

What the Exercises Are For

The XBX will improve your general physical condition by (1) increasing muscle tone; (2) increasing muscular strength; (3) increasing muscular endurance; (4) increasing flexibility; and (5) increasing the efficiency of your heart. Each exercise is included because of its contribution in one or more of these areas.

The first four exercises are primarily to improve and maintain flexibility and mobility in those areas of the body which are usually neglected. They also serve as a warm-up for the more strenuous exercises which follow.

Exercise Five is for strengthening the abdominal region and the muscles of the fronts of the thighs.

Exercise Six exercises the long muscles of the back, the buttocks, and the backs of the thighs.

Exercise Seven concentrates on the muscles on the sides of the thighs. These muscles get very little work in routine daily activities, or indeed in most sports.

Exercise Eight is primarily for the arms, shoulders, and chest, but at the same time exercises the back and abdomen.

Exercise Nine is partly for flexibility in the waist area and for strengthening the muscles of the hips and sides.

Exercise Ten, the stationary run with jumping, while exercising the legs, is primarily for the conditioning of the heart and lungs.

The two supplementary exercises are included for those who wish to do a little more. One exercise is for strengthening the muscles of the feet and the ankle joint. The other is for those muscles of the back and abdomen which assist in the maintenance of posture.

What the Charts Mean

Below is an explanation of what the chart pages mean. Check the paragraph headings with the sample chart on page 47.

Exercise

The numbers across the tops of the charts are the exercise numbers from 1 to 10. The column headed 1 refers to Exercise One, and so on. The exercises are described and illustrated in the four or five pages following each chart. Exercises 8A and 8B are the supplementary exercises described on pages 72–4. If you choose to do these, do them between Exercises Eight and Nine.

Level

The numbers along the left side of the chart are the levels of the programme, and each refers to the line of numbers beside it under the
exercise headings. For example at Level 14 you do Exercise Three seven
times, Exercise Six fifteen times, and so on.

Minutes for Each Exercise

The allotted time for each exercise is shown here. The exercises numbered 1 to 4 are the warm-up and all four are to be completed within two
minutes, or about a half minute each. Other examples: Exercise Five
takes two minutes and Exercise Six take one minute. The total time for
each level of ten exercises is twelve minutes. It is important that all the
exercises be done within this total time limit. Do not move up to the next
level until you can do your present level, without excessive strain or
fatigue, in the twelve minutes.

Recommended Number of Days at Each Level

Record in the box provided on each chart page the number of days it is
recommended that you spend at each level before progressing to the
next. (See instructions for using the plan on pages 48–9.)

My Progress

This chart is provided to enable you to keep an accurate record of your
progress on the way to your physical fitness goal. Record the dates you
started and finished each level. Make a note of how you felt as you did
the exercises. To use the bottom chart, select a reasonable aim for
yourself in terms of body measurements and record this in the boxes
marked 'My aim'. Then record your present measurements on the
Start line. When you have completed the exercise chart, note your latest
measurements on the line labelled Finish. The finish line on one chart
will be the start line on the next.
Note: do not expect startling results. Fitness takes time and persistence.
Couple your X B X programme with a good diet, and your progress will be
steady.

Sample chart

			EXERCISE											
		1	2	3	4	5	6	7	8	9	10		8A	8B
	24	15	16	12	30	35	38	50	28	20	210		40	36
L	23	15	16	12	30	33	36	48	26	18	200		38	34
	22	15	16	12	30	31	34	46	24	18	200		36	32
E	21	13	14	11	26	29	32	44	23	16	190		33	29
	20	13	14	11	26	27	31	42	21	16	175		31	27
V	19	13	14	11	26	24	29	40	20	14	160		28	24
	18	12	12	9	20	22	27	38	18	14	150		25	22
E	17	12	12	9	20	19	24	36	16	12	150		22	20
	16	12	12	9	20	16	21	34	14	10	140		19	19
L	15	10	10	7	18	14	18	32	12	10	130		17	15
	14	10	10	7	18	11	15	30	10	8	120		14	13
	13	10	10	7	18	9	12	28	8	8	120		12	12
Minutes for each Exercise		2				2	1	1	2	1	3		1	1

Recommended number of days at each level [ ]

MY PROGRESS			
LEVEL	STARTED	FINISHED	COMMENTS
24			
23			
22			
21			
20			
19			
18			
17			
16			
15			
14			
13			

	DATE	HEIGHT	WEIGHT	WAIST	HIPS	BUST
My Aim						
Start						
Finish						

Your Fitness Goal

As is explained in the instructions for the use of the programme on pages 48–9 each age group is given a physical fitness goal to attain; that is, a level which they should try to reach.

The goals indicated in this plan are based on the average achievements of girls and women who have participated in it. Your goal, then, is the level of fitness that the average girl or woman of your age reached without undue stress, strain, or fatigue.

With every average, there are individuals who surpass it, and those who fall below it. In terms of the XBX plan and the goals, this means that there will be some women who are capable of progressing beyond the goal indicated, and on the other hand, there will be persons who will never attain this average level.

If you feel able to move further through the charts than your goal, by all means do so. If, on the contrary, you experience great difficulty in approaching this level you should stop at a level which you feel to be within your capability. It is impossible to predict accurately a level for each individual who uses this programme. Use the goals as guides, and apply them with common sense.

From time to time as you progress through the levels you may have difficulty with a particular level or exercise. If so, proceed slowly but keep working at it. (These 'plateaux' may occur anywhere in the progression.) Generally you will be able to move ahead after a few days at this level. If you cannot, then you have probably arrived at your potential physical fitness level in so far as this particular programme is concerned.

Caution

If for any reason you stop doing XBX for more than two weeks because of illness, vacation, or any other cause – do not restart at the level you had attained before stopping. Do drop back several levels or to the next lower chart until you find a level which you can do fairly easily. Physical fitness is lost during long periods of inactivity. This is particularly true if the inactivity is caused by illness.

Instructions for Using the XBX Plan

First select your goal for your age from the table below. Locate this level in the charts which follow. Mark it in some way – circle it or underline it.

Record the recommended minimum number of days at each level in the box provided on each chart page. For example if you are 28 years of age, your goal is Level 30 on Chart Three and you spend at least two days doing each level on Chart One, three days at each level on Chart Two, and five days at each level on Chart Three. Do not move faster than the recommended rate.

If your age Is (years)	Your goal is Level	Recommended Minimum Number of Days at each Level on			
		Chart One	Chart Two	Chart Three	Chart Four
7–8	30	1	1	2	x
9–10	34	1	1	2	x
11–12	38	1	1	2	3
13–14	41	1	1	2	3
15–17	44	1	1	2	3
18–19	40	1	2	3	4
20–25	35	1	2	3	x
26–30	30	2	3	5	x
31–5	26	2	4	6	x
36–40	22	4	6	x	x
41–5	19	5	7	x	x
46–50	16	7	8	x	x
51–5	11	8	x	x	x

To Start and Progress

Start at Level One, which is at the bottom of Chart One. When you can do this level without strain and in twelve minutes move up to Level Two. Continue through the levels and charts in this way until you reach the goal level recommended for your age group, or until you feel you are exercising at your maximum capacity.

When You Reach Your Goal

Once you have reached your goal you should require only three exercise periods a week to maintain it.

Chart 1

	LEVEL	1	2	3	4	5	6	7	8	9	10	8A	8B
						EXERCISE							
L	12	9	8	10	40	26	20	30	14	14	170	18	20
	11	9	8	10	40	24	18	28	13	14	160	17	18
	10	9	8	10	40	22	16	26	12	12	150	16	17
E	9	7	7	8	36	20	14	24	10	11	140	14	15
	8	7	7	8	36	18	12	20	9	10	125	13	14
V	7	7	7	8	36	16	12	18	8	10	115	11	12
	6	5	5	7	28	14	10	16	7	8	100	10	11
E	5	5	5	7	28	12	8	14	6	6	90	8	9
	4	5	5	7	28	10	8	10	5	6	80	7	8
L	3	3	4	5	24	8	6	8	4	4	70	6	6
	2	3	4	5	24	6	4	6	3	3	60	5	5
	1	3	4	5	24	4	4	4	3	2	50	4	3
Minutes for each Exercise		2				2	1	1	2	1	3	1	1

Recommended number of days at each level [1]

MY PROGRESS

LEVEL	STARTED	FINISHED	COMMENTS
12	8·14	8·21	7 mins – fine
11	9·30	9·39	9 mins – fine
10	11·00	11·07	7 mins – fine
9	9·00	9·07	7 mins fine
8	12·49	12·57	8 mins – fine
7	12·49	12·56	7 mins – fine
6	12·14	12·21	7 mins – fine
5	12·31	12·37	6 mins – fine
4	2·20	2·27	7 mins – fine
3	12·30	12·36	6 mins – fine
2	11·44	11·50	6 mins – fine " " "
1	11·45	11·51	6 mins – fine but breathle

	DATE	HEIGHT	WEIGHT	WAIST	HIPS	BUST
My Aim	7 1 85	5ft 2½	8st 5lb	25-25½	35½ in	35½ in
Start	27/12/85	5ft 2½	8st 8lbs	26 in	35½ in	35½ in
Finish	7 1 86					

Chart 1

Exercise One. Toe touching

Start Stand erect, feet 12 inches apart, arms over head.

Bend forward to touch floor between feet. Do not try to keep knees straight. Return to starting position.

Count Each return to starting position counts one.

Exercise Two. Knee raising

Start Stand erect, hands at sides, feet together.

Raise left knee as high as possible, grasping knee and shin with hands. Pull leg towards body. Keep back straight throughout. Lower foot to floor. Repeat with right leg. Continue by alternating legs – left then right.

Count Left and right knee raises count one.

Exercise Three. Lateral bending

Start Stand erect, feet 12 inches apart, hands at sides. Keeping back straight, bend sidewards from waist to left. Slide left hand down leg as far as possible. Return to starting position and bend to right side. Continue by alternating to left then right.

Count Bends to the left and right count one.

Exercise Four. Arm circling

Start Stand erect, feet 12 inches apart, arms at sides. Make large circles with left arm. Do one quarter of total count with forward circles and one quarter with backward circles. Repeat with right arm.

Count A full arm circle counts one.

Exercise Five. Partial sit-ups

 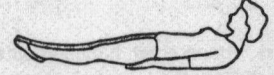

Start Lie on back, legs straight and together, arms at sides.

Raise head and shoulders from floor until you can see your heels. Lower head to floor.

Count Each partial sit-up counts one.

Exercise Six. Chest and leg raising

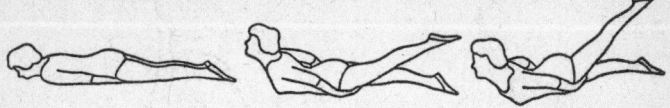

Start Lie face down, arms along sides, hands under thighs, palms pressing against thighs.

Raise head, shoulders, and left leg as high as possible from floor. Keep leg straight. Lower to floor.
Repeat raising head, shoulders, and right leg.
Continue by alternating legs, left then right.

Count Each chest and leg raise counts one.

Exercise Seven. Side leg raising

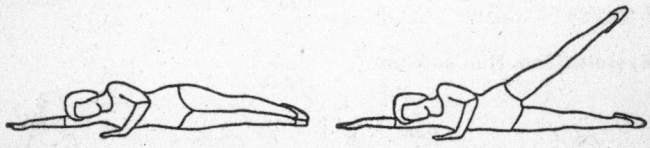

Start Lie on side, legs straight, lower arm stretched over head along floor, top arm used for balance.
Raise upper leg 18 to 24 inches. Lower to starting position.

Count Each leg raise counts one. Do half number of counts raising left leg. Roll to other side and do half number of counts raising right leg.

Exercise Eight. Push-ups

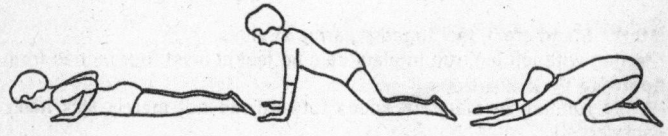

Start Lie face down, legs straight and together, hands directly under shoulders.

Push body off floor in any way possible, keeping hands and knees in contact with floor. Sit back on heels. Lower body to floor.

Count Each return to starting position counts one.

Exercise Nine. Leg lifting

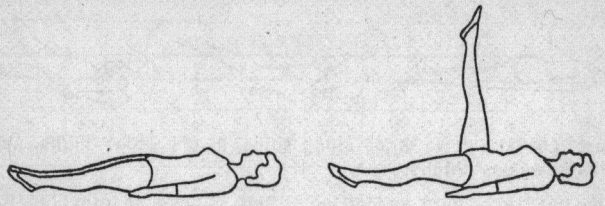

Start Lie on back, legs straight and together, arms at sides, palms down.

Raise left leg until it is perpendicular to floor, or as close to this position as possible.
Lower and repeat with right leg.
Continue by alternating legs, left then right.

Count Left plus right leg lifts count one.

Exercise Ten. Run and hop

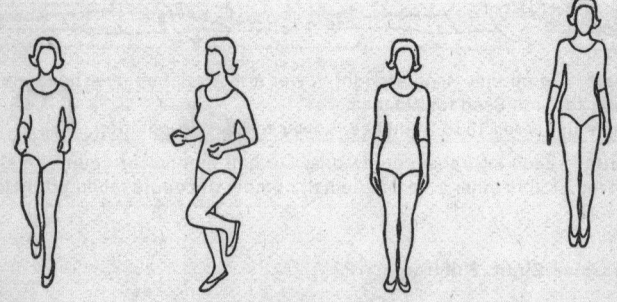

Start Stand erect, feet together, arms at sides.
Starting with left leg, run in place raising feet at least four inches from floor.
(When running in place lift knees forward, do not merely kick heels backwards.)

Count Each time left foot touches floor counts one.
After each fifty counts do ten hops.

Hops Hopping is done so that both feet leave floor together. Try to hop at least four inches off floor each time.

Note: In all run-in-place exercises only running steps are counted towards completing exercise repetitions.

Chart 2

			EXERCISE										
		1	2	3	4	5	6	7	8	9	10	8A	8B
	24	15	16	12	30	35	38	50	28	20	210	40	36
L	23	15	16	12	30	33	36	48	26	18	200	38	34
	22	15	16	12	30	31	34	46	24	18	200	36	32
E	21	13	14	11	26	29	32	44	23	16	190	33	29
	20	13	14	11	26	27	31	42	21	16	175	31	27
V	19	13	14	11	26	24	29	40	20	14	160	28	24
	18	12	12	9	20	22	27	38	18	14	150	25	22
E	17	12	12	9	20	19	24	36	16	12	150	22	20
	16	12	12	9	20	16	21	34	14	10	140	19	19
L	15	10	10	7	18	14	18	32	12	10	130	17	15
	14	10	10	7	18	11	15	30	10	8	120	14	13
	13	10	10	7	18	9	12	28	8	8	120	12	12
Minutes for each Exercise		2				2	1	1	2	1	3	1	1

Recommended number of days at each level [2]

MY PROGRESS			
LEVEL	STARTED	FINISHED	COMMENTS
24			
23			
22			
21			
20			
19			
18			
17			
16			
15			
14			
13	9.43	850	Finns Line

	DATE	HEIGHT	WEIGHT	WAIST	HIPS	BUST
My Aim						
Start						
Finish						

Chart 2

Exercise One. Toe touching

Start Stand erect, feet 12 inches apart, arms over head.

Bend forward to touch floor between feet.
Bob up and down touching floor a second time.
Return to starting position.

Count Each return to starting position counts one.

Exercise Two. Knee raising

Start Stand erect, feet together, arms at sides.

Raise left knee as high as possible grasping knee and shin with hands.
Pull leg against body. Keep back straight throughout. Lower foot to floor.
Repeat with right leg. Continue by alternating legs – left then right.

Count Left and right knee raises count one.

Exercise Three. Lateral bending

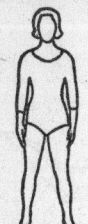   

Start   Stand erect, feet 12 inches apart, hands at sides.

Keeping back straight, bend sidewards from waist to left. Slide left hand down leg as far as possible. Bob up a few inches and press sidewards and down again.
Return to starting position and repeat same movements to right side. Continue by alternating to left then right.

Count   Bends to left and right count one.

Exercise Four. Arm circling

Start   Stand erect, feet 12 inches apart, arms at sides.

Make large circles, with both arms at same time, backwards and round. Do half the number of repetitions making backward circles and half making forward circles.

Count   Each full arm circle counts one.

Exercise Five. Rocking sit-ups

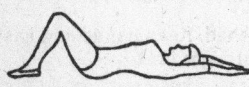  

Start   Lie on back, knees bent, feet on floor, arms extended over head.

57

Swing arms forward and at same time thrust feet forward and move to sitting position. Reach forward, trying to touch toes with fingers. Return to starting position.

Count Each return to starting position counts one.

Exercise Six. Chest and leg raising

Start Lie face down, arms along sides, palms pressing against thighs

Raise head, shoulders, and legs as high as possible from floor. Keep legs straight. Return to starting position.

Count Each return to starting position counts one.

Exercise Seven. Side leg raising

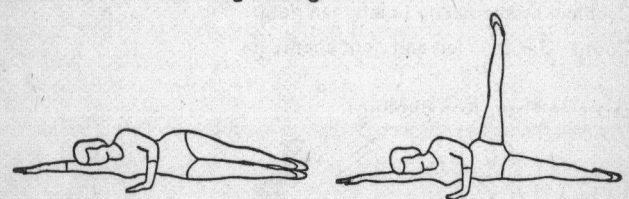

Start Lie on side, legs straight, lower arm stretched over head along floor, top arm used for balance.

Raise upper leg until it is perpendicular to floor or as close to this position as possible. Lower to starting position.

Count Each leg rise counts one. Do half number of counts raising left leg. Roll to other side and do half number of counts raising right leg.

Exercise Eight. Knee push-ups

Start Lie face down, legs straight and together, hands directly under shoulders.

Push body off floor until arms are straightened. Keep hands and knees in contact with floor. Try to keep body in straight line.

Count Each return to starting position counts one.

Exercise Nine. Leg-overs

Start Lie on back, legs straight and together, arms stretched sidewards at shoulder level.

Raise right leg to perpendicular. Drop it across body, and try to touch left hand with toes. Raise leg to perpendicular and return to starting position. Repeat same movements with left leg. Keep body and legs straight throughout, and shoulders on floor.

Count Each return to starting position counts one.

Exercise Ten. Run and stride jumping

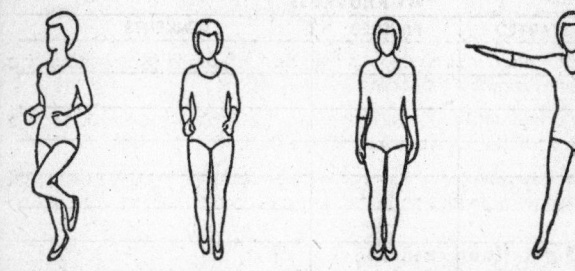

Start Stand erect, feet together, arms at sides. Starting with left leg run in place raising feet at least four inches from floor.

Count Each time left foot touches floor counts one.

After each fifty runs do ten stride jumps.

Stride jump Stride jump starts with feet together, arms at sides. Jump so that feet are about 18 inches apart when you land. At the same time as you jump, raise arms sidewards to shoulder height. Jump again so that feet are together and arms are at sides when you land.

Chart 3

		EXERCISE											8A	8B
		1	2	3	4	5	6	7	8	9	10		8A	8B
L	36	15	22	18	40	42	40	60	40	20	240		32	38
	35	15	22	18	40	41	39	60	39	20	230		30	36
	34	15	22	18	40	40	38	58	37	19	220		29	34
E	33	13	20	16	36	39	36	58	35	19	210		27	33
	32	13	20	16	36	37	36	56	34	18	200		25	31
V	31	13	20	16	36	35	34	56	32	16	200		24	30
	30	12	18	14	30	33	33	54	30	15	190		23	28
E	29	12	18	14	30	32	31	54	29	14	180		21	26
	28	12	18	14	30	31	30	52	27	12	170		20	25
L	27	10	16	12	24	29	30	52	25	11	160		19	23
	26	10	16	12	24	27	29	50	23	9	150		17	21
	25	10	16	12	24	26	28	48	22	8	140		16	20
Minutes for each Exercise		2				2	1	1	2	1	3		1	1

Recommended number of days at each level [3]

MY PROGRESS

LEVEL	STARTED	FINISHED	COMMENTS
36			
35			
34			
33			
32			
31			
30			
29			
28			
27			
26			
25			

	DATE	HEIGHT	WEIGHT	WAIST	HIPS	BUST
My Aim						
Start						
Finish						

Chart 3

Exercise One. Toe touching

Start   Stand erect, feet about 16 inches apart, arms over head.

Bend down to touch floor outside left foot. Bob up and down to touch floor between feet. Bob again and bend to touch floor outside right foot. Return to starting position.

Count   Each return to starting position counts one.

Exercise Two. Knee raising

Start   Stand erect, feet together, arms at sides.

Raise left knee as high as possible, grasping knee and shin with hands. Pull leg against body. Keep back straight throughout. Lower foot to floor. Repeat with right leg. Continue by alternating legs – left then right.

Count   Left and right knee raises count one.

Exercise Three. Lateral bending

Start   Stand erect, feet 12 inches apart, right arm extended over head, bent at elbow.

Keeping back straight, bend sidewards from waist to left.
Slide left hand down leg as far as possible, at the same time press to left with right arm.
Return to starting position and change arm positions. Repeat to right.
Continue by alternating to left then right.

Count   Bends to left and right count one.

Exercise Four. Arm circling

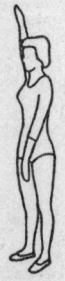  

Start   Stand erect, feet 12 inches apart, arms at sides.

Make large circles with arms in a windmill action – one arm following the other and both moving at same time. Do half number of repetitions making backward circles and half making forward circles.

Count   Each full circle by both arms counts one.

Exercise Five. Sit-ups

Start Lie on back, legs straight and together, arms along sides.

Keeping back as straight as possible, move to a sitting position.
Slide hands along legs during this movement finally reaching forward
to try to touch toes with fingers.
Return to starting position.

Count Each return to starting position counts one.

Exercise Six. Chest and leg raising

Start Lie face down, legs straight and together, arms stretched sidewards at shoulder level.

Raise entire upper body and both legs from floor as high as possible.
Keep legs straight. Return to starting position.

Count Each return to starting position counts one.

Exercise Seven. Side leg raising

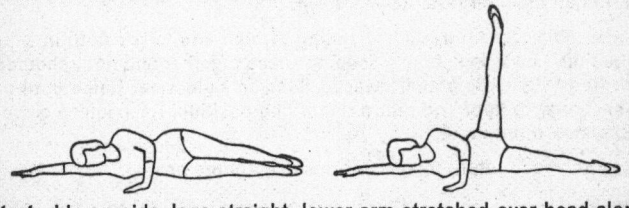

Start Lie on side, legs straight, lower arm stretched over head along
floor, top arm used for balance.

Raise upper leg until it is perpendicular to floor. Lower to starting
position.

Count Each leg raise counts one. Do half number of counts raising
left leg. Roll to other side and do half number of counts raising right leg.

Exercise Eight. Elbow push-ups

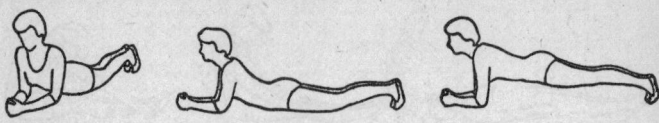

Start Lie face down, legs straight and together, elbows directly under shoulders, forearms along floor, and hands clasped together.

Raise body from floor by straightening it from head to heels.
In the up position, body is in a straight line and elbows, forearms, and toes are in contact with floor. Lower to starting position. Keep head up throughout.

Count Each return to starting position counts one.

Exercise Nine. Leg-overs – Tuck

Start Lie on back, legs straight and together, arms stretched sidewards at shoulder level, palms down.

Raise both legs from floor, bending at hips and knees until in a tuck position. Lower legs to left, keeping knees together and both shoulders on floor. Raise legs and lower to floor on right side. Raise until perpendicular to floor and return to starting position. Keep knees close to abdomen throughout.

Count Each return to starting position counts one.

Exercise Ten. Run and half knee bends

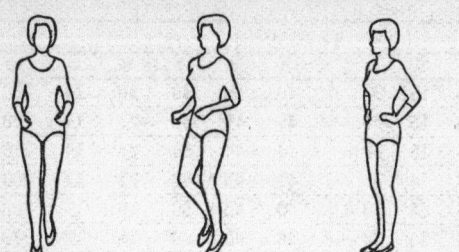

Start Stand erect, feet together, arms at sides.

Starting with left leg, run in place raising feet at least six inches from floor.

Count Each time left foot touches floor counts one.
After each fifty counts do ten half knee bends.

Half Knee bends Half knee bends start with hands on hips, feet together, body erect. Bend at knees and hips, lowering body until thigh and calf form an angle of about 110 degrees. Do not bend knees past a right angle. Keep back straight. Return to starting position.

Chart 4

				EXERCISE							
		1	2	3	4	5	6	7	8	9	10
	48	15	26	15	32	48	46	58	30	16	230
L	47	15	26	15	32	45	45	56	27	15	220
	46	15	26	15	32	44	44	54	24	14	210
E	45	13	24	14	30	42	43	52	21	13	200
	44	13	24	14	30	40	42	50	19	13	190
V	43	13	24	14	30	38	40	48	16	12	175
	42	12	22	12	28	35	39	46	13	10	160
E	41	12	22	12	28	32	38	44	11	9	150
	40	12	22	12	28	30	38	40	9	8	140
L	39	10	20	10	26	29	36	38	8	7	130
	38	10	20	10	26	27	35	36	7	6	115
	37	10	20	10	26	25	34	34	6	5	100
Minutes for each Exercise				2		2	1	1	2	1	3

Recommended number of days at each level ☐ 4

MY PROGRESS			
LEVEL	STARTED	FINISHED	COMMENTS
48			
47			
46			
45			
44			
43			
42			
41			
40			
39			
38			
37			

	DATE	HEIGHT	WEIGHT	WAIST	HIPS	BUST
My Aim						
Start						
Finish						

Chart 4

Exercise One. Toe touching

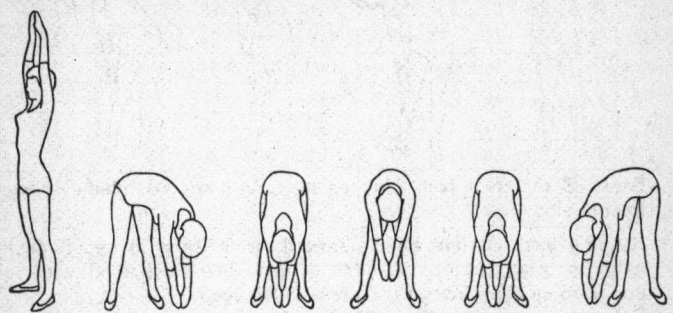

Start   Stand erect, feet about 16 inches apart, arms over head.

Bend down to touch floor outside left foot. Bob up and down to touch floor between feet. Bob again touching floor between feet once more. Bob and bend to touch floor outside right foot.
Return to starting position.

Count   Each return to starting position counts one.

Exercise Two. Knee raising

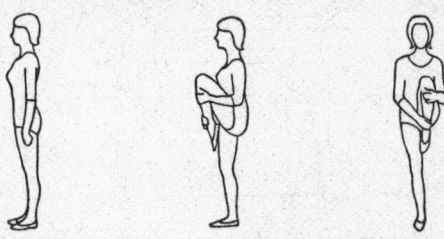

Start   Stand erect, feet together, arms at sides.

Raise left knee as high as possible, grasping knee and shin with hands. Pull leg against body. Keep back straight throughout.
Lower foot to floor.
Repeat with right leg. Continue by alternating legs – left then right.

Count   Left and right knee raises count one.

Exercise Three. Lateral bending

Start Stand erect, feet 12 inches apart, right arm extended over head, bent at elbow.

Keeping back straight, bend sidewards from waist to left. Slide left hand down leg as far as possible, at same time press to left with right arm. Bob up a few inches and press to left again.
Return to starting position and change arm positions.
Repeat to right.
Continue by alternating to left then right.

Count Bends to left and right count one.

Exercise Four. Arm flinging

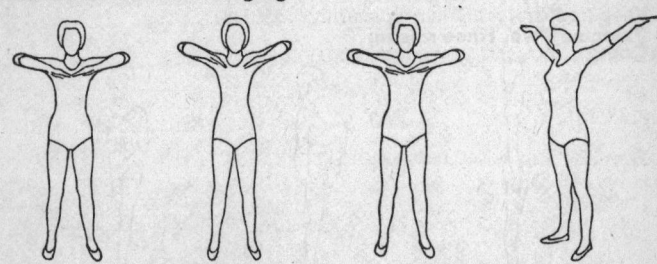

Start Stand erect, feet 12 inches apart, upper arms extended sidewards at shoulder level, elbows bent, outstretched fingers touching in front of chest.

Press elbows backward and upward. Do not let elbows drop.
Return arms to starting position and then fling hands and arms outward, backward, and upward as far as possible.
Return to starting position.

Count Count one after each arm fling.

Exercise Five. Sit-ups

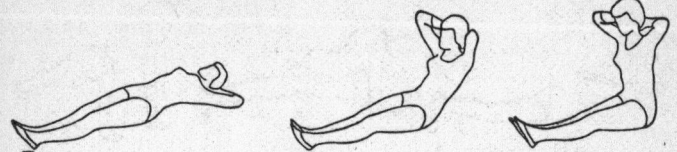

Start Lie on back, legs straight and together, hands behind head.

Move to sitting position. Keep feet on floor (support may be used if necessary) and back straight. Lower body to starting position.

Count Each return to starting position counts one.

Exercise Six. Chest and leg raising

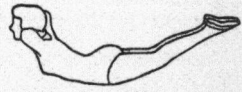

Start Lie face down, legs straight and together, hands behind head.

Raise entire upper body and both legs from floor as high as possible. Keep legs straight. Return to starting position.

Count Each return to starting position counts one.

Exercise Seven. Side leg raising

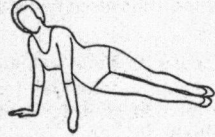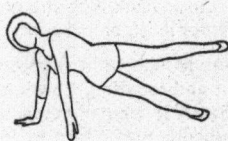

Start With right side to floor, support weight on right hand (arm straight) and side of right foot, using left hand for assistance in balance if necessary.

Raise left leg until it is parallel with floor. Lower leg to starting position.

Count Each leg raise counts one. Do half number of counts raising left leg. Change to other side and do half number of counts raising right leg.

69

Exercise Eight. Push-ups

Start Lie face down, legs straight and together, toes turned under, hands directly under shoulders.

Push up from hands and toes until arms are fully extended.
Keep body and legs in a straight line. Return to touch chest to floor and repeat.

Count Each time chest touches floor count one.

Exercise Nine. Leg-overs – Straight

Start Lie on back, legs straight and together, arms stretched sidewards at shoulder level, palms down.

Raise both legs until they are perpendicular to floor, keeping them straight and together. Lower legs to left, trying to touch left hand with toes. Raise to perpendicular and lower to right side. Raise again to perpendicular and return to starting position.

Count Each return to starting position counts one.

Exercise Ten. Run and semi-squat jumps

Start Stand erect, feet together, arms at sides.

Starting with left leg, run in place raising feet at least six inches from floor.

Count Each time left foot touches floor counts one.
After each fifty counts do ten semi-squat jumps.

Semi-squat jumps Drop to a half crouch position with hands on knees and arms straight. Keep back as straight as possible, one foot slightly ahead of the other. Jump to upright position with body straight and feet leaving floor. Reverse position of feet before landing, return to half crouch, and repeat.

Supplementary Exercises

On this page and the following two pages the supplementary exercises for feet, ankles, and posture are illustrated and described. If you wish to do these exercises they are to be included in your regular programme between Exercises Eight and Nine and are numbered Eight A and Eight B.

Chart One

Supplementary Exercise Eight A. Feet and ankles

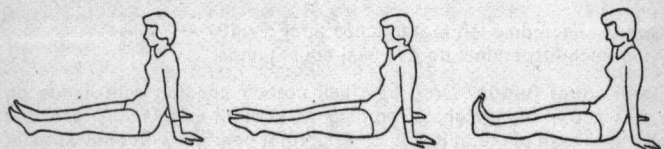

Start Sit on floor, legs straight and about six inches apart, hands behind body for support, feet relaxed.

Press toes away from body as far as possible. Bring toes towards body hooking feet as much as possible. Relax feet.

Count Each return to relaxed state counts one.

Supplementary Exercise Eight B. Posture

Start Sit on floor, knees bent, feet on floor, hands clasped about knees, head bent forward, and body relaxed.

Straighten body and lift head to look directly ahead. Pull in muscles of abdomen. Relax to starting position.

Count Each return to starting position counts one.

Chart Two

Supplementary Exercise Eight A. Feet and ankles

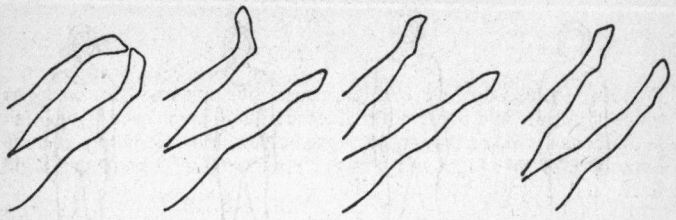

Start Sit on floor, legs straight and heels about 14 inches apart, hands behind body for support, feet relaxed.

Move feet so that toes make large circular movements. Press out and around and in and towards the body. Do half number of counts moving toes in one direction, then reverse for remainder of counts.

Count Each time toes describe a full circle counts one.

Supplementary Exercise Eight B. Posture

Start Lie on back, knees bent, feet on floor, arms slightly to side. Relax muscles of trunk.
Press lower part of back to floor by tightening muscles of abdomen and back. Relax to starting position.

Count Each return to starting position counts one.

Chart Three

Supplementary Exercise Eight A. Feet and ankles

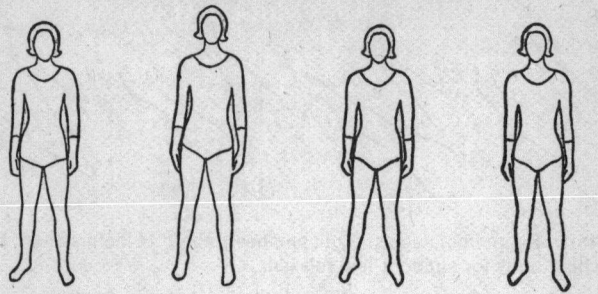

Start Stand erect, arms at sides, feet about 12 inches apart.

First raise up on to toes, then lower until feet are flat on floor.
Next roll outward on sides of feet, then roll feet so that outside edge of
foot is off floor. Return to starting position.

Count Each return to starting position counts one.

Supplementary Exercise Eight B. Posture

Start Lie on back, legs straight and together, arms slightly to side.

Relax muscles of trunk.
Press lower part of back to floor by tightening muscles of abdomen and
back. Relax to starting position.

Count Each return to starting position counts one.

FIND OUT MORE ABOUT
PENGUIN BOOKS

We publish the largest range of titles of any English language paperback publisher. As well as novels, crime and science fiction, humour, biography and large-format illustrated books, Penguin series include *Pelican Books* (on the arts, sciences and current affairs), *Penguin Reference Books*, *Penguin Classics*, *Penguin Modern Classics*, *Penguin English Library*, *Penguin Handbooks* (on subjects from cookery and gardening to sport), and *Puffin Books* for children. Other series cover a wide variety of interests from poetry to crosswords, and there are also several newly formed series – *Lives and Letters*, *King Penguin*, *Penguin American Library*, and *Penguin Travel Library*.

We are an international publishing house, but for copyright reasons not every Penguin title is available in every country. To find out more about the Penguins available in your country please write to our U.K. office – Dept EP, Penguin Books Ltd, Harmondsworth, Middlesex UB7 0DA – unless you live in one of the following areas:

In the U.S.A.: Dept DG, Penguin Books, 299 Murray Hill Parkway, East Rutherford, New Jersey 07073.

In Canada: Penguin Books Canada Ltd, 2801 John Street, Markham, Ontario L3R 1B4.

In Australia: Marketing Department, Penguin Books Australia Ltd, P.O. Box 257, Ringwood, Victoria 3134.

In New Zealand: Marketing Department, Penguin Books (N.Z.) Ltd, P.O. Box 4019, Auckland 10.

In India: Penguin Overseas Ltd, 706 Eros Apartments, 56 Nehru Place, New Delhi 110019.

The Massage Book

George Downing

With this simple manual you can practise and perfect the art of massage.

The instructions, which are clearly illustrated and easy to follow, detail the strokes and positions to be adopted for massaging every part of the body from the top of the head to the tips of the toes.

George Downing, who is an expert in a style of Swedish massage now widely used in California, discusses the advantages of using oil or powder, explains the difference between working on the floor or with a table and suggests the kinds of speed and pressure your hands should maintain.

Massage is an act of healing and a powerful means of communicating without words. In order to convey the full range and effect of the art, the author outlines its wider 'philosophy' and its links with oriental cults. He includes, too, chapters on meditation and on massage for lovers.

Skin and Hair Care

Edited by Linda Allen Schoen

What is the best treatment for acne?
How safe are eye cosmetics?
What causes dandruff?
Would plain lanolin make a good night cream?
Can oral contraceptives cause hair loss?
Is there a danger of skin cancer from using a sun lamp?
Do rejuvenating creams really eliminate wrinkles?

These and literally hundreds of questions of daily concern to everyone are answered in the three parts of this handbook along with questions about such special topics as birthmarks, excessive hair, and aesthetic surgery.

This Slimming Business
John Yudkin

John Yudkin is Professor of Nutrition and Dietetics at the University of London and here gives authoritative advice about slimming and draws the lines between fact, fashion, and fad.

Although a good deal of nonsense is printed in some women's magazines about slimming, Professor Yudkin shows in this readable and often entertaining handbook that the effort involved in carrying extra weight can be harmful and may lead to a number of ailments, some fatal. For other than merely fashionable reasons, therefore, it is wise to watch your weight – without being too impressed by the so-called average weight tables – and, if necessary, to take sensible steps to reduce it.

This Slimming Business is not heavy reading. Light verses by Ogden Nash help the author's easy style to keep the weight well down.

How to Lose Weight Without Really Dieting
Michael Spira

1 Lose weight without crash dieting, counting calories or feeling hungry and irritable.

2 Re-educate yourself so that you are both slim *and* healthy.

3 Eat your favourite cream bun and still keep the svelte outline – whatever your age.

4 Learn about the constituents of food and how they affect weight and health.

How to Lose Weight Without Really Dieting debunks current slimming fads and fallacies, offering instead a sensible scientifically based programme of eating that will help even the weakest-willed to take off weight. Michael Spira realizes that if you love rice pudding you are not likely to really give it up and, taking this into account, he shows you how to establish successful eating patterns which, with only a little self-control, will last you for the rest of your life.

In short, Dr Spira tells you how to have your cake and eat it.

The Complete Book of Running

James E. Fixx

'This book is a boon and a blessing to the multitudes who jog and run throughout the world' – Michael Parkinson

As the title says, this is The Complete Book of Running, the best book yet written on running for those who run, would like to run, have ever run or are just curious about running.

Fixx explains why runners feel better, live longer, enjoy a more vigorous life, sleep better and smoke and drink less than their sedentary friends.

This is the complete book, and so is of use to the beginner and the experienced runner alike. Anecdotal and filled with information, the book contains advice for runners of all ages, men, women and children. Here is the guide to all running, from first steps to total fitness.

Sailing

Peter Heaton

Fifth Edition

Sailing offers everything a sport should offer – fun, excitement and satisfaction.

This handbook caters for the beginner. It describes the techniques of choosing, buying, fitting out, sailing and storing a yacht, in detail and in simple language. In addition there are shanties, salty stories, sea-lore, instructions on subjects ranging from weather forecasting to the cure of seasickness, and the whole is profusely illustrated with line drawings and photographs.

Sailing has proved its solid worth by remaining in print for thirty years, during which Peter Heaton has regularly revised the text and brought points of detail up to date. In this latest edition he has incorporated the 1976 revision of the Collision Regulations and the new Buoyage System, as well as much new technical information and a whole lot of new drawings.

Keep in Vogue with Penguins

Vogue Guide to Skin Care

Keep every inch of the skin of your body in glowing health! Here the Beauty Editor of *Vogue* shows you where your skin is most vulnerable, when to get expert advice; analyses facial types; describes proper cleansing, freshening and moisturizing and the changes that age brings; and discusses specialized problems. There is a whole section on total body care – diet, exercise, depilation, hands and feet, tanners and protectors – written to help you understand what causes and alleviates skin troubles, plus an A–Z of common skin problems.

Vogue Guide to Hair Care

The book for everyone who wants glossy, healthy hair! Here you can find out about your hair's structure and type, what happens to it with age, and how to look after it. The author advises you on finding a style to suit you and to keep you looking your best – whatever the weather. There is detailed advice on colouring with natural and man-made dyes, on permanent waving and straightening, and on styles for special occasions, wigs and hairpieces. And, as diet affects hair, the guide includes useful recipes, an A–Z of hair care, plus an illustrated glossary of recent cuts and styles.

Vogue Guide to Make-up

Your make-up routine and the equipment you'll need is detailed for you here, whatever your colouring or skin type, whatever the lighting, climate or time of day. Here are illustrations with expert advice to show you how to do it, plus notes on what to wear with what, how to make the most of your best features and guidelines for the different age-groups. There's also an A–Z of scent terms and, to add the final polish, twelve steps to a professional pedicure, tips on how to choose your nail colour and how to varnish your nails.

Also in Penguin by Georgina Howell

Vogue Body and Beauty Book
Vogue Natural Health and Beauty

Also in Penguin by Barbara Tims

Vogue Book of Diets and Exercise